MICHAEL JACKSON
Instrumental Solos

Arranged by BILL GALLIFORD, ETHAN NEUBURG and TOD EDMONDSON

Produced by
Alfred Music Publishing Co., Inc.
P.O. Box 10003
Van Nuys, CA 91410-0003
alfred.com

Printed in USA.

ISBN-10: 0-7390-7799-6
ISBN-13: 978-0-7390-7799-3

CONTENTS

Song Title	Page No.	CD Track Demo	Play Along
TUNING NOTE (B♭ Concert)			1
BEAT IT	4	2	3
BILLIE JEAN	6	4	5
BLACK OR WHITE	8	6	7
DON'T STOP 'TIL YOU GET ENOUGH	10	8	9
HUMAN NATURE	12	10	11
I JUST CAN'T STOP LOVING YOU	14	12	13
THE WAY YOU MAKE ME FEEL	16	14	15
SHE'S OUT OF MY LIFE	18	16	17
WILL YOU BE THERE (THEME FROM "FREE WILLY")	20	18	19
MAN IN THE MIRROR	22	20	21
THRILLER	24	22	23
YOU ARE NOT ALONE	26	24	25

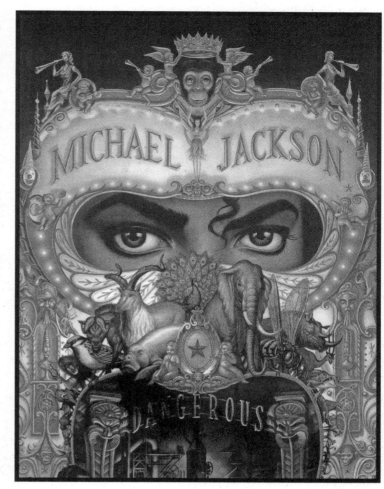

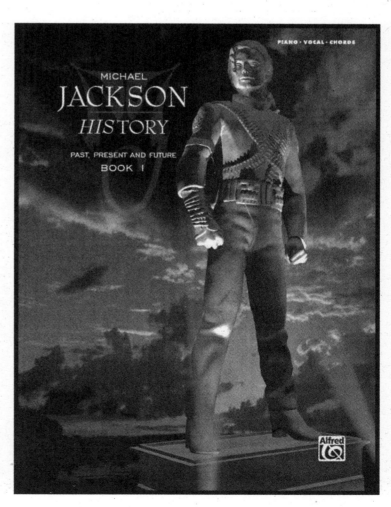

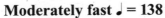
Track 2: Demo
Track 3: Play Along

BEAT IT

Written and Composed by
MICHAEL JACKSON

Moderately fast ♩ = 138

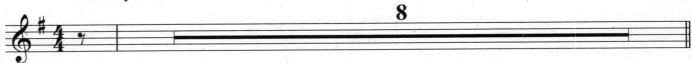

Beat It - 2 - 1

BILLIE JEAN

Track 4: Demo
Track 5: Play Along

Written and Composed by
MICHAEL JACKSON

Billie Jean - 2 - 1

BLACK OR WHITE

Rap Lyrics Written by
BILL BOTTRELL

Written and Composed by
MICHAEL JACKSON

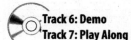
Track 6: Demo
Track 7: Play Along

Optional Rap:

(Spoken:) Protection for gangs, clubs, and nations,   causing grief in human relations.

Black or White - 2 - 1

It's a turf war,   on a global scale.   *I'd rather hear both sides of the tale.*

You see, it's not about races, just places,   **faces. Where your blood comes from is where your space is.**

I've seen the sharp get duller,   *I'm not going to spend my life being a color.*

DON'T STOP 'TIL YOU GET ENOUGH

Track 8: Demo
Track 9: Play Along

Written and Composed by
MICHAEL JACKSON

Moderate dance tempo ♩ = 112

Don't Stop 'til You Get Enough - 2 - 1

HUMAN NATURE

Track 10: Demo
Track 11: Play Along

Words and Music by
JOHN BETTIS and JEFF PORCARO

Human Nature - 2 - 1

I JUST CAN'T STOP LOVING YOU

Track 12: Demo
Track 13: Play Along

Written and Composed by
MICHAEL JACKSON

I Just Can't Stop Loving You - 2 - 1

Chorus:

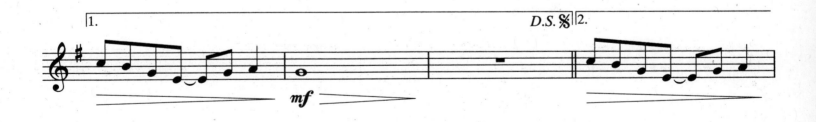

I Just Can't Stop Loving You - 2 - 2

THE WAY YOU MAKE ME FEEL

Track 14: Demo
Track 15: Play Along

Written and Composed by
MICHAEL JACKSON

Moderate shuffle rock ♩. = 112   *Verse:*

Chorus:

The Way You Make Me Feel - 2 - 1

To Coda

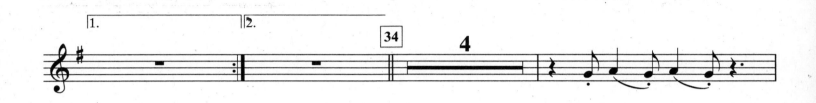

D.S. % al Coda

Coda

SHE'S OUT OF MY LIFE

Track 16: Demo
Track 17: Play Along

Words and Music by
TOM BAHLER

Slowly, with expression (♩ = 72)

She's Out of My Life - 2 - 1

WILL YOU BE THERE

Written and Composed by
MICHAEL JACKSON

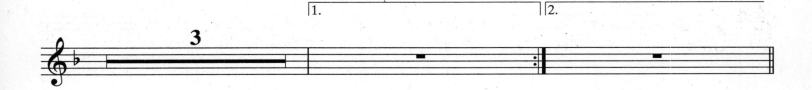

Will You Be There - 2 - 1

MAN IN THE MIRROR

Words and Music by
SIEDAH GARRETT and GLEN BALLARD

Track 20: Demo
Track 21: Play Along

Man in the Mirror - 2 - 1

THRILLER

Track 22: Demo
Track 23: Play Along

Words and Music by
ROD TEMPERTON

Thriller - 2 - 1

Track 24: Demo
Track 25: Play Along

YOU ARE NOT ALONE

Words and Music by
R. KELLY

31 *Chorus:*

39

PARTS OF A TRUMPET AND FINGERING CHART

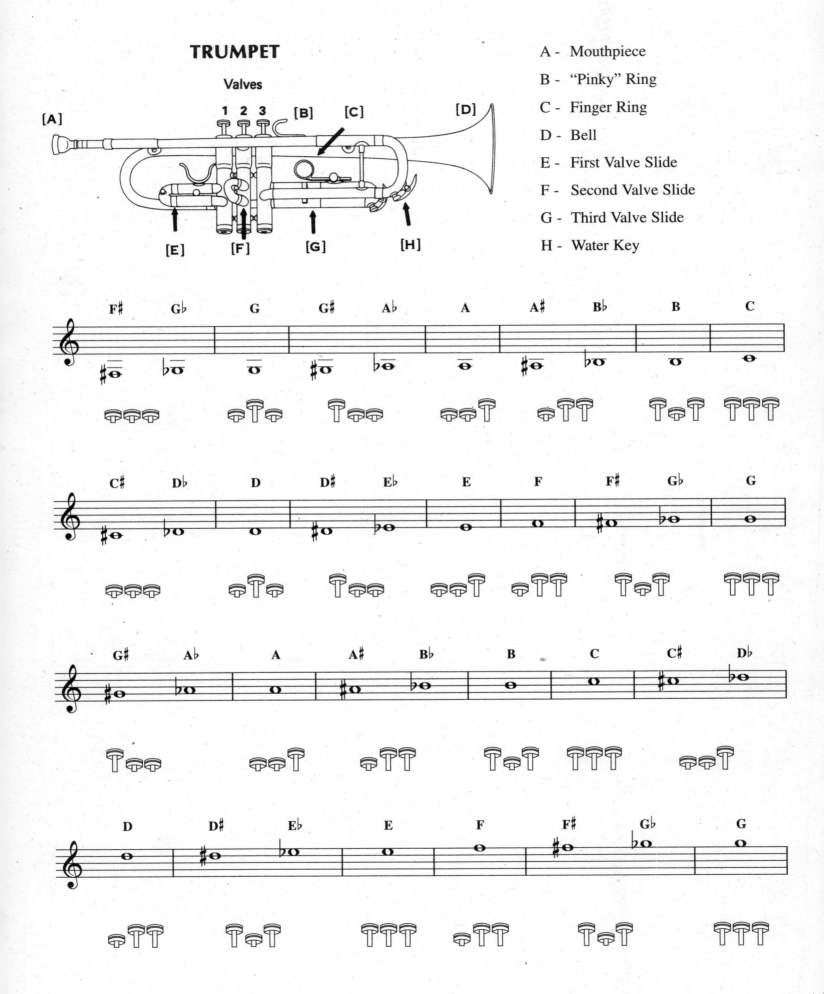